the bentleys

THE UNIVERSITY OF ALBERTA PRESS

the bentleys

Dennis Cooley

Published by

The University of Alberta Press
Ring House 2
Edmonton, Alberta, Canada T6G 2E1

LIBRARY AND ARCHIVES CANADA CATALOGUING IN PUBLICATION

Cooley, Dennis, 1944-
    The Bentleys / Dennis Cooley. — 1st ed.

(Currents)
Poems.
ISBN-13: 978-0-88864-470-1
ISBN-10: 0-88864-470-1

    1. Prairie Provinces—Poetry.   2. Depressions—1929—Prairie Provinces—Poetry.
I. Title.   II. Series: Currents (Edmonton, Alta.)

PS8555.O575B45 2006   C811'.54   C2006-905873-3

All rights reserved.
First edition, first printing, 2006.
Printed and bound in Canada by Marquis Book Printing Inc., Montmagny, Quebec.

A volume in (currents), a Canadian literature series, Jonathan Hart, series editor.

The University of Alberta Press is committed to protecting our natural environment.
As part of our efforts, this book is printed on Enviro Paper: it contains 100% post-
consumer recycled fibres and is acid- and chlorine-free.

The University of Alberta Press gratefully acknowledges the support received for
its publishing program from The Canada Council for the Arts. The University of
Alberta Press also gratefully acknowledges the financial support of the Government
of Canada through the Book Publishing Industry Development Program (BPIDP)
and from the Alberta Foundation for the Arts for its publishing activities.

   Canada Council   Conseil des Arts
          for the Arts   du Canada

for my prairie friends Birk, David, Bob, Wayne
and in memory of Sinclair Ross

Some of these poems have appeared,
often in different versions,
in *it's still winter, Beyond Borders,*
the bentley poems, and *West Coast Line.*

⚜

"I suppose, if we knew how,
we could dance a little just
ourselves out here."

—Sinclair Ross, *As for Me and My House*

the bentleys

that's what the playbill says you say
  the duckbill platypus too
    as luck would have it
                    yes there is
a big grin plastered all over your face
and it is hung in a locket from your dreams

    as a matter of fact you are
looking you've got your eye
    out for someone
really important this is
    don't knock it eh
                    what i have to realize
                someone in my place
      it isn't easy
            it has to be someone
                    who can read
        this stuff
no way this can be an imposter
      sashaying in on a sway
back pockets full of wind and dust

      listen why did i always ask
all these questions why did i have to pester
                    you you are counting
        on me some one
    whose heart is really in it
someone to climb from
        four-postered dreams
                past heavy dreams
someone who could care about this country
would jump onto the paper as it went by
ride off on it to camels and clowns

anyone who might comb the burrs out of sleep
a person who would want to play her part

& in part you are
trying that is
you really are
quite preposterous
prosperous too with outlandish stories
if i might say so
making quite a go
of it quite the pro
position right from the word go

WIND AND HORSES

WIND AND HORSES

a puritan tale of romance and intrigue
set in the dirty thirties

a stirring drama that dares
to ask the question
can a woman find happiness
as the wife of a small-town minister
as keeper of journal & lover
    in:
         full black & white
         full view
         full frontal

Dramatis Personae:

—Phyllis Mae Alison Bertha McPhyllips as:
    Phyllis: anguished wife of Philip, erstwhile lover of Paul
—The Tormented Author as:
    Philip: torn between wish and refusal
—The Muse as:
    Judith: pale figure, a voice like the wind,
    taken with Tormented Author
—The Poet as:
    Paul: lover of puns & muses, a sneaky little guy
—The Readers as:
    sun dry others, they have their parts
—The Horses as:
    horses
—Jimmy Ross as:
    dennis cooley: author of THE BENTLEYS

every evening the sun rips
                    open on the edge of horizon
torn open by sharks some say
    it bleeds brightly

        eases into a
soft suffusion of iodine
which spreads in the water
until night begins

        an inkwell spilled
        where we reach
the rorshach of our dreams
spreads and thickens
blots out the blood

        quickly turns into blacktop
            crows swagger across
                big-shouldered
        think they are poets
            smelling the dark

            in black-leather jackets
    they tack loudly across morning
their hobnails clacking on the linoleum light

                    tick tick tick no
          this is not grasshoppers
          not glasses nor a motor
          cooling in heat
          nor is it a clock

                              says look phil
                    paul at the blackboard
                    so worn little sticks to it

          quick flecks of chalk
          what's he doing, paul
          what does he think this is
                    school or what
          & why won't he play
          hookie that is me im good
          and ready for skipping out

          look phil & there are two
          hearts crossed over & above that
          my god our faces at night

          something aghast something
          desperate little sticks
          spared only their sharpness
          the way the board
          thank god shrugs
          off their edges
          they are flaking away
          already, our faces
          phil's & mine

small light from our window
swish of rain
there is something flannel
& warm blankets
soft gurgle & drip

drip _{*drip*} something
in us too i suppose
leaking, lacking maybe
baby with the croup, next door, coughing
scratchy wood we wind our love over
itchy as wool as quick to snag

falls on the spots fluent
as a sax o
phone the rain

as mellow & as achingly
beautiful philip the wet
ribbons yellow with crayon
me a funnel the music runs through
the wooden floor the sounds
round us in a bowl &
you can smell the earth
—plums, or is it musky
& i think of fennel the smell of curry
remember how carraway feels
wishing i could be
carried away

the window a great emptiness
blind as a mirror
when no one is there

                    mrs. b. you say
                    mrs. b. this is
               sign language
and it may be

strange gestures we make
                    jesters we are
          to one another
                         jesus what seems
slow movements of hands
                    & fingers
bodies drowning   in air

there should be a sign
what we want
                    are signs

                    our bent &
          stuttering
bodies

what can we say
          to one another

               we all hear the flutterings
                    in wind

how utterly alone we are
                    each to each
old people in a home
            we have lost
                    our children
            we are children
                    cannot find
the place they keep

                    words & let them
            out from a long winter
crazy as cattle in spring

shoved under covered up covered over
our homes shipped from one square
to another shudder across the mercator
our lives abbreviated and held in check

God leans over and makes
                              the moves
          God knows all
the moves God knows he does
knows yours too

                    buccanneers of love
          in your checkered and abdicated lives
               looking for rain

from which to string lines
across the curving and dirty earth
God tapping his feet and keeping time
God on his fiddle plays with rhyme meddles with time
plays til the end with a ferocity that leaves him
          red-faced and
                              gasping for air

          we ourselves are
                              getting closer
          we are frogs crossing to water a lot of us
stomped by cows before we make it

to the other side where we were
promised on arrival we would all be

kings and queens crowned
          in the conflagration
that is one big barn dance

wanting always abundance
      the abduction of flesh

  all night we carry on
  a wild bone dance
  one last chance

              the last post
            past everything
        pushed over the burning
edge of the world

this is love in an arid land
the heat so unbearable /love too
                              burns

          your feet barely able to move
          seek camouflage in not moving
                wait for the end
the red ruin on the horizon
the black arabian a man in silk
      voice loud in opera
where in the meantime she grows
irascible as a camel that's come up lame

this is the parable the one true story
the world that seemed to live before us
like chenille she limps over
stinking & spitting & testy
everywhere beset by tsetse flies

it is loud and vile-tempered, the world
and leads across air so hot and droning
it stretches all day until
      it turns to carmel
and the whole sky is drowning

says you know it's almost chique
& you you handsome devil
you could be the sheik of araby
himself you really could

& she well she was prepared
she would be ready to stop scratching
she would do almost anything
                if need be to lift her face
out of the burning sands &
                        like Nefertiti lie
            with me
or if not Nefertiti
                    Aida then

a bluff of poplars   by the ravine
under the sour smell of leaves
        the thick waxen skins
burrs on the stems where they will break
listening to a stiff wind
    the dusty rattling clouds scudding
the saskatoons turning purple
        dusted with heat
here on this side of the rise
            its small shelter

    light   /shadow
                        /light

envelopes in which we send ourselves

always at the door always
at the door when I am riding

Paul she calls *Pa-auull*

voice rises slightly on her toes
and there is a small half wave
   lake when a boat passes
smiles as if she doesn't know /a waif

        will anyone
   wave back

     Harlequin foolish-faced
      stops knows
    he stops
       here
   he is in a romance
 someone else has written

Paul on his way to somewhere

tear the corner off the 19th
century & there it is
this ladies' home
journal in four-colour wallpaper &
terracotta jugs painted
blue & green benches &
listen everything you will say
you will have said before so listen
there 's this little dog
—eared laugh a kink in air
a crinkle you can't iron out
but you know you have heard

she cries out at night
when she dreams
you are with her
or that you are not

the skins we are sealed & sent
in & then
many people
they are hands in the street waving

good-bye bye   bye they say
hundreds of arms & hands
on the other side of flutter

never fail they all fluster when they look
flour-pale faces tied over their chins
the wrinkles their eyes wear uncertain
as chatelaines holding torn linen
their bodies become stems the stern
knowledge flesh is storming
up &   escaping

their lives escarpments
        they want to fall off
     scrape themselves all the way down

            they are turning purple
        turn the corner
            the page & there
                        they are
                again
        god forbid
     all the faces wobble
        & there you are
                    turning the page
            florid from impatience

rags theyre oily rags philip
says when i tell him

                    fine in the or
y mr p. reacher but
the crows are getting into the garbage
and I am in one of my rages

                  only they seem to be
                      laughing, too
                  the crows

        they've wiped up night & now
        it's our turn he shrugs
                only i think
        well he likes them

                the crows
      at their age
                the stupid things
spitting on the feet of winter

however outrageous they may be or old
   cronies over stoves & stories
might have been crayoned there charcoal
as the pot-bellied heaters they sit around
   vigilant preachers at their posts

        & i think they must be
   chaperones of some sort fine chaps
      rigged out in those
anachronisms of theirs

      they walk the line

does he like how they shout
obscenities rude insults
small men in black fed up
the world is so white
& so cold

rubs his eyes takes a deep
                          breath &
fills   /
            our eyes our ears nostrils
fills us up dust and earth seeping
      wind & fire sweeping

      a little more
he says poignantly i thot so we grow
darker carrying the brunt of this
                  a burnt light he adds
      calls it sienna though i think
                  he is putting on airs
      especially when he says
                  he has no time Toulouse
      he's gotta get Gauguin
                                  it's pretty
                  elemental really
            we could show a little more
      gratitude he thinks we are pigmies
      pigments of his imagination
      we wouldn't even be in the picture
            it wasn't for him

      seems to have reached an impasse
                              but then
            coloured oil
            he mixes & daubs
      leans over to blow on us
                                  pains
            takingly
                        rubs our eyes
                        takes our breath

      away at night a lull

wind bright the stars bitter
everything thickens with oil
a shine on us almost of water

he's grown more and more persistent
impasto he says smirking
        the cunning linguist
the Lindquists wide-eyed with his talk
but not me im not impressed
not in the least i think he's
really laying it on thick
nothing but dabs & smatters

                              still life
                          he calls us

CIRCA 1933

says this is no circus in case we didn't know

                oh this is impossible philip
& you you are an imposter plain & simple
        not that it matters
don't bother him quit pestering why don't i

brushes sepia thoughtfully into the room
the ochre in the curtains spreads
        certain as the world's sins
all over hell's half acre you could say

                        he sighs bends over slowly
        signs his name

    not much he says
        wiping something out of our eyes
                            / or his

                    you gotta admit
                        it ain't no great hell
                                        but it's
        still life
                                    isn't it

                        we could allow him
                        that much at least
    couldn't we

                    yes I do do
              put it on the line
              do be do be do be
                              oh do be
                       good to me

       haul their wet weight out
       morning pulls it out & twists
              all the cold water
       wrings it dry & sun presses
       flattens their wrists like a roller

    · when I've taken them down
       dozens of gray tongues left behind
       sit flapping on sun & wind
       right beside the out
       house the shameless things
       sun no more than a pint sealer by then

              & when you do
          pop pop
                       buttons come off right left
                                 & centre
       (bout time somebody sent 'er)
       happy as peas shucked

       clothes pins sit there, smirking
       more confident in their lack of paint
       than sparrows & as lewd Paul says
       they are the birds of love, the sparrows
       & straight & narrow's the way

i think that's rude but like it anyway
I say that many well
what's stopping us
c'mon open the door
oh please don't spare us
prepare us by all means prepare the way

except knowing they are
privy to our most intimate secrets
they can't wait the wooden tongues
want more than anything to string us a line
they want to get the dirt on us
squeeze all the dirt they can
out of our laundry
say ah first
chance they get

heard the one about the cowboy

no what

you heard me
no i din't what
what about the cowboy
you heard me
sd the cowboy
to the steers
sd the cowboy
under stars

you hurt me
real bad he sang
me & my steers
muh heifers & me
me & muh heifers
& this here
this here
's what i call
muh hurtin' song

cowboy practices his lines
cowboy clears his throat throws
a few lines out they fall around yr neck
they are not throwaway lines
though they seem to be
lines he bloops out :

But in her book she wrote in pride
Sighed to note the window's pried
Wide open & how hard he'd ride
      And sing his silly head off
All winter lied and all night long
Cried Cowboy Kirby loud with song
She hurt him bad she done 'im wrong
Spit & coughed his rough red cough.

YUK YUK YUKYUK

the stars hurtling overhead
    their milkiness
the sun boiling away toiling
among its sunspots in teapots
electricity crackling with sugar
the cowboy tuned his song
the cowboy turned in his silk
bandana a blue flame in her blue
blue mirror at night
when the room fell back
when nothing filled her
black widow window but
                the stranger
      come to visit her
   loneliness
       slim banana as smooth

when she dreamt all night long
him & her him & her them there
all night long her hemin' & him hawin'
with nothin' but
the music on now
ain't that sweet
he said in her
dream in her

        needless to say
        needles to say
      this was the lady
      the part I played
      i played the part
    THOU SHALT NOT

                                    crooners:
                  those plashy ink pots
                  they've dipped their feathers in again
                  you can spot them   coming
                  the words   dripping out reedy
                          notes from a clarinet
                  letters their thin legs let out
                  all over the dance floor
                  the toenail sounds of love
          everyone there adores crow loves
          the sweet clarity of his voice the need
                          never to blot

at night composed composing
crow flows is a fountain
pen writes the page open
his poor heart purged
wide open is his age is
showing in winter & the sky
a page he puts his foot
prints on the slow way he prances
prince of the praxis the axis
he dances his loneliness on

                                    the winds begin to gust &
                                              rub until they
                              wear away the pages of our hopes

              it begins to go
              bits of earth too
        lift off in gritty crumbs

                    god leans back and
              flicks
                  the back of his fingers
                                    across the page

                  leans over
        fields and yards in a blur
                                disappear

            our lives whisk away
                        on a hot august wind

Philip the terrible sentence
he is under wonder will he
ever escape will he ever
tug on a silk cape singing
hallelujah louder than a choir
yank his charcoal threads
inside out turn the whole works
the whole seanced waiting into
wings & swing past

the coma that calms him
the corrals his proper grammar
shrivels in rigid as coral will he
leap out of correctness with a yawk
thumb his nose at the sun
all the links sighing at his feet
he giggling & wiggling
his comma toes now he loves
to stretch them & how he throws
his lines out dopey as a lariat

a jar of saskatoons with oak cakes
the sheen & the purple
                              smell of musk

        feel your body its pale waiting
        where we peel off the black
                    clothes night dresses us in
                sober as an under
        taker or a preacher taken
        a shine to you and we

                would do well as we
                please ourselves perfume the room
                perform what small steps
                        we know a few tunes
sobre as methodists on sunday morning
        pleats eager in reticence to be
        undone stepping in between
                the sabres
            those that lie there
                        sharp tongues
waiting for one false step

you could have me in stitches
        or out/
        if you aren't careful
                    it's amazing

        grace i hang p.
over us a small cave in
discretion it carves out
        the months ahead

                        turns them
                bowls on a lathe

                    we crave somehow plead
                      the careful way we try
                      the curves the smell
                            your body
              makes on mine

          small moment we can bring in
      importunate as the Portuguese for cod
              could if we wished
          gaze at the world more ~~vacant~~
                vagrant than geese
          don't tell me you didn't notice them
          dragging sonnets across the horizon
                            // twice a year
                            there & back

      out of sight out of time
      p. almost always out
              of time

                    at times I think
                  they must be
        eyes /caught in my head
              my mind frozen
        pigeons stare from can
              not see the fear
              ungodly as sun

                                    flowers ript
                                    out of van
                                    gogh's eyes

    sometimes I think I paint it
    there as if it were
    a sudden wash or bleach
        /   a gash a gouge
    the pain I wish were
    a bit gaudy we are so plain

            I do not mean
              to complain
                  but we are
                  you know,
                        we surely are

dreamt of you philip
       you & i
everything drying
          the whole world dying

       philip i say
the keeping of the house house
keeping i am the house
keeper and the garden
growing our first baby blown out
at first for a few days a soft bottle we blew
                    open & into
shape of our youth the winds slammed shut

                 the door we cradled
      wind an electric garden
      an insect a bright light it was
                 that dry
      & red & black ones
      crawl in & out of the cracks

      some of them are big & blue
      a sun you might have painted
      philip smeared across it
      your bright pain
      so wet it was irridescent, indecent almost

      & there was i thinking raspberries
       in my hands i offer you
      only they are bleeding, all over
) the belly the pig
             hands sticky & screaming

      —never mind you said there are other
      dances & you try to hoe dirt over them
      only the ground is so hard you

can't & there is a sliver
in your hand i try to remove

& then in the dream we heard
the edge of the garden

crr-

aACKK
the gash in the air
sky a stomach ript &

sudden crush of rain
cold so cold
i almost
can't
breathe

dear god the water
all over
my clothes so wet i
might have been
ashamed
only i
wasn't i

was watching water
pouring into the cracks
& you   /against me philip
stiff as a
shiver stiff as
ever you were

& after, the wet wind
the whole garden
a room of ice
a dead robin
red blood on a white cloth

the rooms
we can
                    enter
        for a
            moment
    hearts in a slow canter
                        air going
    slightly off centre

        birds at a feeder
        a small conspiracy p.
            a breathing too ,to
                    gether now
        that it counts
    piracy of air
        their red mouths
            eating
    our breath
            p.
    we do not
breathe a word
        do not
        touch a
                    thing

sometimes feel i am
in an audition for love
for your love you love
your own erudition a standing
oh and in addition **O**
vation you say is what
you deserve sal
vation you deserve better
it's a matter of appreciation
and air   that too
air you diction
we should feel nothing
but elation feel awed
to be in your production
you tell us
in practiced voice we could be
wowed by all we owe you

nothing odd about it you say
you are the director
aren't you don't you
help us through
our lines give us all the best
lines where do we think
they come from if it isn't for you
& your audacity you
brook no contra
diction do everything
by the book
you wrote it
yourself you know
how it should turn out
how we should read it

& now you have visitors you have
visions of bigger things

say you got a lot of moxy
maisie you say maisie
'm gonna pu'chu in the moo-Vees
freckles & all   eyelashes too

you mooch on our hopes seldom if ever listen
dont give me one measly thought
tough you say that's tough but ive got to
learn my part & you pick lint off your sleeve
         your best serge suit
what kind of air you dishin' out
    mister insist i must

          pro^{-ject} my self

         listen this may only be rehearsal
         you say but soon it will be the Real Thing
         it is through me you say i will find u
         you have spoken & that is why
             you have to throw

                                     your voice

                     don't i realize you
             are a ventriloquist
         tous les mondes tous les vents know
         the four winds the seven
         seas swerve through
         they're to open the vents
         you are beezing in
         you are full of it

)& i know your views are well aired
             & isn't it about time
                     it is isn't it
                     & isn't it
                     about time
                     we got a break
         shouldn't we find kisses and make-up

long reach of the arm
bone in its pink case
wings they call lungs
line the inside
cushion the rack of bones

thin bones in the arm
the tibia the fibula
lift them out of the crate
they've slept their lives in
let them out let them scrape
themselves raw
let them
create a little something

play let them
fiddle around &
bow let them
dance once
they've left
the past
they have been
creased or cast in

i suppose we might
dance a little
if only we
could

nothing left
my love
but dance

all the bones
jingling the flesh
a carafe of spirits

meshed together
the leg bones
keeping time hip
bones the ulna
the radius circle
tip, step
oh do not
do not e-
ver stop

these things we hold

and yes my dear
husband beloved
steven darling paul
the three of you
beloved is all

i can do to say
the four of us
it would be too

much to be with
out jude
to be that
daring

it is all true   /every
thing they said these are
we live in
pinched times
and a pall has fallen
a parcel of light has crashed
in our rooms a chair
has broken like a pencil

all I can do is i toss stones
think if this were somewhere
we were in & it is breaking
                    apart

yes yes say the words so fast
& so quick she
                must
          know she must
        know I look
away when she says
              his name
me then those times those eyes

      painted lady i always wanted
to be but dared not say

      those pictures
                it was
          like he had
      taken those
              brushes &
touched me
              with them
      touched me
                himself

                        real hot
            you know it was
                  so gentle & so
      much he wanted

                    and i touched too
          touched where he
              touched
          wanted what
he wanted
                    whatever you think
          and it was me
              there
                         i could feel
          him & i
                         turned
red yearned green turned
into whatever he touched
blue horse in a windy night

              he sees me
                         so much so much
                              of me i am
              ascared

          some times it takes
     everything to say
hello   oh hello
and everything bashes against the barndoor
   the way he takes me away &
     all the hot spots
   that talk to me
   when i am alone

                         who is this man
                         i take away
                              within me

why is it
i must be
untouched
by life
untutored as snow

white with abstinence you would have me
turn my skin
disappear behind
the windows more costly than cold
veins in my breasts blue as skim milk
blouse a bruise on my body

it is parchment you want
me scraped clean
all the words   others, my own
brown and parched

this is some kind
ness you show me my husband
you want me also
perfect in complexion
offer me the blizzard of your inattention

snow   white
a faceless face
a marked up page
on which you write over & over
suspicious notes

gougings of pencil & pen
stencil me my mine mine mine there
staple a serial of fear & anger
& sometimes you stand like a sentinel
smear big greasepencil numbers on brown paper

smell of absinthe on your breath
                    why you ask why do you do that
                              the words in my face
                                 curdled as whey
                    absinthe you say absinthe
                       maketh the heart go
                          marketh the heat
              the love you have learned
                       to mime over & over
the circuit you work year in and year out
         sparks snapping down the line
down my backbolne when i hear you

                                   this happens
                    winter sucks our bones
        threatens with freezer burns

              once there was abundance & we would
         swish in our bodies once there was sun
         we held buzzing
                    in our hands
                 burning in bed

sometimes think i can sink
into long dreams of origin
so unending they say
where they are slung
pole to pole

a lowness on the horizon
it could be smoke or dust
settlers boil in under the sun
there is a blue vapour
exhalations from the past
right out of the blue they hit you
thunk thunk thunk

who woulda thunk
& later the wooden trees
the white & yellow flesh
drying into resonance
their thick stupid trunks
clouds of sparrows snap like clothes
pins on rows of little keys
click click click click
playing Liszt or Chopin
& later become transformers
turn on their sorrowing
their small wings
swing inside

their talk distinct as nails
your words butcher knives
you throw every day
thud thud thud thud
pin me to the spinning world
this is what you call eros
my ears growing
distance on your face

                              behind me marks on the wire
where it's stretched & stitched
flies whap whap whap cling to the screen
crazed with the hot smells of music
they're quizzical with desire ready to throw them
selves into the silly novels you have hung
the sticky curls of their syntax dangles from the ceiling
flies rev their small hot engines at the door

sometimes feel i am
in an audition for love
hoping to win your love

love in a dry land

sometimes that & sometimes

the bentleys

the playbill says you say
you are looking for someone
want someone to play the part

imagine you there in the auditorium
the echoes of its emptiness
wonder if you will hear me
        if you will give me
        the role if i can
        win the part
        i most want

when you say my god you are
one beautiful woman and
i say you have learned your lines
well that's what you do
isn't it & you say well
no as a matter of fact

when they open the planetarium
every night turn the lights on
    the sky frozen with stars
that's when the show gets on the road
that's when big things start to happen

                              & there I'd be
                  smackdab in the middle
                  id be in the movies
                              strange spiders all over
                  the place salamanders
                  luminous with impatience
                  live in fire they say
            the woman saw in my hand

            & you'd say is this fun really
            c'mon admit it
                        this silver fame
            you love it don't you
            you all aflame & tucked
            into a frame that comes & goes

                        fun I'll say you bet
            shades of Hades is what
            & you can't beat that
            you can't beat that
                                          can you

                              puts on an uncertain smile
)thinks i am carried away—

            this is & why not
                  why would I ever
            come back
            except to check the mail
            heck I could rub quiet all over   it's good
            myself & never come back, ever   for the sin
            except I am married   it is
                  to whom I am not   a sign
            sure more mired than admired
                  than May in this unmonied and unmany world

　　　　　　　　though I haven't a clue
　　　how ever like birds we might fling open

　　　　　　　　　　　　　　　　　the doors to
　　　　　　　　　　　　　　　　　wind &
　　　　　　　　　　　　　　　　　flesh

　　　　　know I belong somehow in this noise
　　　　　　　　　　　　　its hot moist traffic
　　　　　the odour of Christmas, our flesh, burning

summer fallowing

                  ssshhh

      sshhh

                it says

        sky a heating pad on yr face

        this is the following summer

        sun sighs

                 & the tired earth

boils over

              sun whispers

    / hawk in the sky

when I am neat
a tidy wrangle of bones
yes I will be still
married to you I will
have eyes for no one
else constant in death

the gold that circles
my drybone finger
my finger still
restless inside
loose vowel
the consonance of your vows

this is not an open
& shut case believe me
not by a long shot

cod liver pills Philip loves oddly
to break in his mouth & chew
a small fragrance i would allow myself
the coolness of lipstick on skin
cool weight of the tubes
you can roll & they are smooth & cool as sin
waxy weight of them and smell
why do I find this
romantic feel so frantic
when the case flops open
an unstuck suitcase

the moment he brushes you so gentle
so by accident of moving it seems
you can never be sure for all
your alarm and wishing it were
you wish the way he holds
shoe laces in his
hand touches brushes
mild as chamomile

he will touch you touch me find me
beautiful feel me through the air
why dont you please Mr Fuller Brush Man
the way small things fly
put out feelers wet threads

don't brush me off
fill me why don't you
with spices & perfume
come from the smallest shifts
dust finds in sun

he moves
cool from his drinking-fountain city
trees & swings & places
you get icecream
the direction he sways

i wish he will touch i can
touch in all the sweet places
far away as a glove
that hurt when we do not
and when we do
hurt me
still

philip singing happily to himself oh buffalo
girls won't you come out tonight come out
tonight come out my pretty little red wing
lays down the wind in dirty dishwater fills it
in long streaks piles heat up around posts
smudges fences into the ground until you
can walk over a sea of dust pure pointillism
all the way a dry slough cracking with paint
we swim with insects through a livid &
liquid sun how does he do it & but you've
got to give the devil his dew given such
touch you could say hey it is pretty slick
thanks he says he 's thinking of calling it

the bentleys

in spring our thoughts like the roads
are barely passable

& then in no time the heat
whap whap
beats dust out of the roads
          sky hangs out
its worn & dirty carpet
god with his hot eye
parsing the seasons
is whacking away at it
                    /at us
as if we were wayward kids

impossible to conceive
to explain such weather, such grunts

except we are born to it
          a patient people
durable as rocks in the northeast
obdurate & implausible in waiting
    in love as unyielding

in the garden he calls
it figures wedge themselves white
as frozen angels blue as english
china they rub through grit all of them
            lean into or away
      you can't tell which

      if you knew the four
winds blow either way they're waving
hi mom so long dad each of us
to & fro below or toward
the frame we are looking for
a way out a ledge to step
where we can flap like pigeons in wind

try to keep the door from blowing
away please philip we say please
don't you know it's us you can't
      just brush us aside
            you can't just up & ignore
            our aches & pains are real
            things have gone haywire
            & here we are no thanks to you
      stuck in ochre mired in umbre

            now you've gone
      & done it you've painted us in
            to a corner &
      what's the point
      we're out of the picture
            darn near

well what is he supposed to do
jude likes it she says it's good
       he's sick & tired of us
who are we to talk
bitching & moaning he could take
umbrage at our age has it ever
dawned on us even once
    he says with a sickly
grin i'm in this too he says stick
with him he's stuck with us
(i think he's stuck on Jude)
through thick & then this is difficult
      why don't we just sit
still a moment why don't we talk
about ingratitude he can take us
      places he can make us
famous make us known
for miles & miles around he reaches
out toward
       the weedy horizon
but what would be the point
all of us here
huffy and indignant as stars in the last judgment

all these nights
bent over my diary

feel like a sparrow
walking on ice

no not a skater
not even that

though I would be
would have that grace
the free speed

their breath beneath their feet
writes behind them

no i'm afraid
i have only

scratchings the smallest
wind could
rub out
sun could melt
in an hour

                    our days are lowered
on hemp from a horizon that
all the way from europe lours
opens now on dawns we louvre up
steep cliffs chapels cathedrals galleries

            on lawns she lays
            before me
            lays for me
                        lays me
            down to sleep
                        by day we man
            oeuvre in dust & chaff
                        rub our eyes
as we go up and down the shaft
become confused angels that hover
      how are we to know
the light filtered through
            the silent moving

when the earth lurches
it launches us into the west
winds we steady ourselves within
                /shaky topoi we
latch onto the ropes sun
                    drops and we tug
pulleys on which night flops
alongside which the winds rise

meanwhile pullets drop their shellacked moons
which form giant pearls inside a huge ocean
                they cover with darkness

it is then we lift a big soft moon into the sky
study the stars where they spill
down the stairs every intermission
        we spray the bright powder
without permission spatter it
                    our breath brightens
                        the dark
                    boards over head &
                    the world begins to shine

spit & squat like a cabbage in this
            scabby place it's scandalous
waiting among crow's yodel, his squabble
                    his broken yellow nails
                    & Philip says let's not get
                            carried away
        shall we
        & he lets go with a squib of complaints

things are getting a little sticky
                granted but
he hacks & slashes the canvas
        I feed him (Ulysses
        sharpening the pencil
        for the big guy's eye
till it turns into spaghetti

        this is no way to talk
        who am i to talk
        & if i know
        what 's good
        for me this is
        i better watch
        my language
        i better hold
        my tongue

                    let up only
            when other
creatures from their own dim planets crash
        the night the moon
                the panels swing
        the small things
                    click
    / / chips in a casino
hit the screen they're big stars
        light up thick with movement
thrash to get inside the sun
where it has travelled & they too
a billion years of light unravel
        stacked in all those plants
burning & brought to this room

she said it passes
through you on the way
to somewhere on & on
it passes all
understanding

it quivers & quavers away
long as Mrs. Lundquist's solo
& she upright
as her piano or almost it seems
though momentary as a mosquito
and why not
it's high time isn't it

takes outlines of your dreams
takes lines out from you

winds them on a big spool
with other lines
a bird making a nest
deft as a man, fishing

it happens to you
& it starts to stick
inside some of it
& then
more & more
& pretty soon
you're full of it

it falls down into your toes
your every dream
takes on calcium talks in phosphorous
the fine lacquer of time, sets

& before you know it
you're all filled up with time
you got great bones & teeth
& you die
she said
that's it she said
you up & die

feel like a vowel
owls emit & sometimes yell
bed sheet so tight no one could move

a wounded self, or lame
in these stories Paul so dapper
when the yard fills up
on the soft yarn of moonlight
could this be our yearning
and he himself winds up in his own
on his way under the big dipper
his pony constant he insouciant
his stories of where things happen
things popping up everywhere
mousetraps going off with a sharp snap
so important i dare not yawn

they don't just up & disappear he says
oh no he says it doesn't add up do not dear
lady despair

try me try me
on for size
one size fits all
seize me this very day
why don't you she says
take it from me
we're in this together
winner take all

it will be telling
i will be telling
this with a sigh
ages & ages hence
why me why not me
think of me
as a shitake mushroom
why don't you you hand
some devil me
first hey shake me why don't you
shake it up why don't you
shake me up huh go ahead
i could go for a darn good
shaking you always thot i cld
use a shacking up

who knows maybe a few notes
will fall out crying maybe if I were
shaken you could hear
melodies cascading
smoother than blue
birds glittery as one
armed bandits broken open
singing their music of coins

if you throw money at me
I will sing you a song of sin
I will glow I will croon

lewder than a wurlizter
and looser   lots looser
my eyes will flash red & gold
you could take me for a whirl
i could be your girl
in blue you could call me
you could throw me for a loop
bloopy as the failed lariat
you whirl around your feet

you really could throw me
off oh i wld be yr poet
laurie et frail with arias
if only you
were to toss
yr heart at my feet
i wouldn't step around
/never   /not me
i would step inside
where the air stops

spin it round & round the hop
scotch smooch smooch steps
you would teach me
if you were to fill me
up on romance pull my arm
as you have been
pulling my leg
just once plug in my nickel
odeon dreams turn me on
in a splash of silver
maybe we could have a little
fun find us a little

hoochie koochie
live in syn
ecdoche /ok?

maybe i could p.
maybe we could
if you wouldn't
always step aside

you could call me
your girl and
i would call you
up i would call you
handsome

& you/ you could call me
any time
night or day

two long rows of rocks side by side
running along the spine of the hill
where it humps south of the slough
water in wet springs ran through

Steve standing and standing there
where he found a bone arrowhead
his eyes look out so far he must see
the whole world and holes in it
out of its skin out of eternity

where they made their camps
must have thought it would never go away

what this must have been once a vast
grass a fox came through and forever
huge world so impossibly large
buffalo in mosquitoes stampeded into never

so silent you must have felt god
hold his breath when you stand
the suns steady pressure the wind
imagine mile after mile sun and sun
sun & wind grass this tall &
                    the tall yellow
flowers in that wind the stars
shining with tipi rings medicine
wheels turtle effigies rubbing stones
          flies & dung & sweat
bluestems right up to the horses bellies
poetry roaring gently in their dreams

when i look in the mirror
faces fall out   appear &
disappear among the black keys
no no not cardboard faces
they are not cupboard either
though they are brittle as bone
white as china, as sour milk
as their breath is all winter
long you can see their breath
the church is so cold

that's the choir, blackly gowned
they make their ragged way
through hymns rise
& sit in thumps & rustles
crows with white heads
old rugged cross, nothing, they
have earned their crowns
I would say they are all mouths
except they are ears too don't I know
ears to the wind as if they
expected the second
coming at any moment

that's me at the organ, playing for glory
that's us paul, that's us philip
clumsy white faces on the prairie
its chained & charcoal night
all that land bleak as when
I think of you dead & me left
together we make what music we can

in scarves & coats
stiffness hangs from us like kids
mittens tied on strings

we cannot shake or leave
all the night melodies we want to play
till night flash-floods our bodies

                    it could be jazz
               it should be blues

old foot-joint that's you
7 or 8 times you shed
your years take on /briefly/
a new sin
spin under a howling & blistered sun
break into song
sky a hot tin
roof only you could walk on
talk about being in heat
going through fire

all our days brought to this
the same old tune
after all this time i can still hear
the song of limbs you sing
rubbing one another like grasshoppers the clumsy four
legged dance you do behind rocks

the one thorny moment
when you
reach
hot sting
more piercing than revelation

yes yes the scalding music i too we two dance
sloughfoot in agony   /or ecstasy
i can't tell which
grateful you have not crushed or torn me
i have not ript the limbs you climb over me upon

i am tempted
to say the rest of the time i duck into mud
or i dig in
fatten up & sleep in
my lady's chamber beneath the frost line

                    don't worry i won't make
                    a move until i see the light
                                of your eyes

            my gasps stored up in comic-strip balloons
    doze for days & days until sun shows up
            yanks the sheets off & gives me a smacker
                    one big warm one

                        but im afraid
        this doesn't   /happen
                no use holding your breath hoping
                    for spring
                            my long-legged prince
                    no sense standing on happen
            stance

                        as it happens
            i wait in the sands for the sands
                        gather`myself in strings
                    watch eternities of insects the world spends
                they stream through the neck of time
                    the nuclear clock we call sky

            i can hear it all now their gossip
            all my days are done they say
    cloaked in muslin soaked in nuclear winter
    ever since wanting to step past all absence all abstinence
    listen for the stumble of your coming
            the terrible disease we call love

where do you go
     phyllis
somewhere behind yourself
     & dust

somewhere behind where
things glue in brown
shadows to the floor
& when you pull them they
     leave a thin film

     the eyes you
        push aside
   curtains
        to look

when darkness
          touches
shine blindly
    behind your locked face
     a softness

in a locket   a valley
    at your breast

to cast a spell
a spelling bee

spell	married	
		admirer
spell	angel	
		glean
spell	angelic	
		lacing
spell	asking	
		as king
spell	fondle	
		enfold
spell	hearing	
		reaching
spell	breast	
		barest
spell	now	
		won
spell	lips	
		slip
spell	finger	
		fringe
spell	skin	
		sink
spell	desired	
		eddies, resided
spell	earthen	
		earneth
spell	sounding	
		undoings
spell	waist	
		waits
spell	arching	
		chagrin

spell	risk
	irks
spell	table
	bleat
spell	meal
	lame
spell	meringue
	regimen
spell	towels
	lowest
spell	please
	elapse
spell	leaps
	lapse
spell	wanting
	waning
spell	tender
	rented
spell	garden
	danger
spell	leafing
	finagle
spell	persimmon
	misnomer
spell	talks
	stalk
spell	secret
	erects
spell	sapiens
	pansies
spell	calls in
	call sin
spell	braid
	rabid
spell	auburn
	urban

spell	spirits
	strips
spell	dances
	ascend
spell	vivavious
	vicious
spell	belated
	bleated
spell	elastic
	laciest
spell	naked
	knead
spell	lasting
	salting, staling
spell	casualties
	casual ties
spell	compliant
	complaint
spell	dreamer
	reamed ·
spell	elation
	toenail
spell	endear
	earned
spell	coddles
	scolded
spell	feeling
	fleeing
spell	companionship
	companions hip
spell	blessed
	bedless
spell	flesh
	shelf
spell	trays
	satyr

spell	joyful	
		foul
spell	whisper	
		perish
spell	happiness	
		penis
spell	confide	
		confined
spell	undress	
		sunders
spell	delirious	
		soured
spell	lovely	
		volley
spell	touch	
		ouch, torch
spell	wines	
		swine
spell	sinew	
		swine
spell	friend	
		finder
spell	equals	
		squeal
spell	marital	
		martial
spell	purest	
		erupts
spell	nudes	
		used
spell	tones	
		stone
spell	deserve	
		severed
spell	live	
		vile, evil

```
spell          mans laughter
                                  manslaughter
spell          dreamer
                         rearmed
```

        spell love philip spell yes spell us
        spell joy spell water spell me
        please spell me off spill joy
says mrs. b. misses may bee

the gray pencils and lines so wobbly
they could have been made
by kids   or drunken farmers

on which commas turn into notes
hang from wires sparrows with their toes
  tune to a pushing wind

He had taken on board
all his loneliness, I
think, or meant to. All
that loneliness a basket
he would ship his
sickness home in.

Pulled the terrible
music of his
homecoming foot by
foot behind him,
enough for any ship,
such yearning could fill
any ship, and they say
it sits there anchored
to sun in the middle of
grass & wind just before
it drops off
the end of
the world.

& you do you look up
through the windy glass
you spot them
trillions upon trillions
high on a hot wind
the terrible beauty of their noise
windy as birds & shrill

somewhere in a theatre called the Rex
Shirley Temple lisps & twinkles
the film clicks & thwacks
darkens & lightens

here they blacken the sky in their passing
the whole earth broken
lighting lanterns all day long

all night long the terrible heat
when the winds run low at last
the silent screams we take to bed
turn our cavernous & windy heads on
instruments waiting for music
cataracts of blood going through
the quick stir in wrists the rest of our bodies
all the wrecked music there

& then   the trestle over the creek
what once was a creek   the sound
the far call   a train
always at night   you hear it
the long lonely sound   it plays from you
& something in you
answers back

on its way   to lovely names
.   it is going to wet places   peaches streams
that lonely whistle   every night
on its way   to somewhere
on its way   to loneliness

hard drizzle of consonants
hear them on the roof
dumb dumb dumb dumb
your mouth speaks under
the thunder & the bendy wind
that's us all right—the Bentleys/
                    We serve & serve.
                       Never swerve.
                          Not once.
                            I swear.

We are so
branded.
                 And do
                 They say
                 Deserve it.

kirby throws you
        for a loop a curve
    a slider a split-finger in
finitive he can really hum it
infinitely he would like you to believe
definitely can he is definitive
in his own loose-limbed way
they say he can wing it with the best
& i believe them & sometimes him
when he stands there the sun clear as resin
when he clears his throat *hh-hmhm* he says
                he can also throw you
    off or out you're not careful
look out here comes a spitter
or maybe not maybe im not
            ready for this
the cunning devil can he turn it loose

thinks he has always something clearly
to prove and so he spits in the dust says
he can make things happen
create something out of nothing
without me he's nothing so help him god
im not there waiting at home

all he is is a sputter a dangling
modifier he is not moderate no he's not
            not by a long shot
& what's more there's no damn way
            he can ever be
better stick with him he's tumbling
his heart up there heaving
        his way into heaven

im welcome to come along
all i gotta do is catch his words

　　must picture me there
staring through the screen
　　　　　　door banging
　　my hands together
　　　begging for what comes next
m'on baby m'on big chucker
all that thumping and smacking

he hunches over peers in
till you think he is about to
　　fall off the mound
fire ball now come to me honey
　　you'ndme now you'ndme

if you must know he gets
wound up a little too much
too often too & once he does he can
really bring it to you he says

it happens you know in the 7th
always did & always will
they haul out the big canvas
& it slithers across the field like a shed skin

every trace of summer vanished
every move the last sign we shared va
moosed wiped out written off
it's beaten it scrammed
off you might say

it's the bottom of the 9th
it's beginning to spatter
they may call the game

and they slide across
                    the small words
you spoke and scratched in your plate
till you'd hardly dare look up
                        afraid to see what he has
                            seen in your hands
                            what he shouts
                            what he reads
                                in the dirt

how is it phyllis
you fill all the room
your pens & your lamp
gives itself off
smoky as perfume
till the night runs dry

all you do
empties me
till i am dry
& silent

a fly when a spider is done

have only this space
   these lines
     you enter &
examine whenever you please

all grist for the secrets
you fold neat as napkins
   inside notebooks
   night after night
you never open to me
any more than the rest
your life you never
     show what is
beneath the binding

where you have drawn
   back the covers
practise your mute regime
the pen & ink & paper

in quest of air you are
putting on airs it's a
question of what
you expect nothing
short of or less than a stellar performance
want dance want flamboyance
though it is only a matineé

THE BENTLEYS

starring:

phyllis may bentley

(and an unsupporting cast of local women & men)

∞ at the galaxy orpheum roxy ∞

NIGHTLY

stoughton estevan lampman

can't help
noticing how she manages

Mr. Finlay who hardly lets
out a peep looks down & grins
sheepish grin plastered
all over his face
when Mrs. Finlay says

if she wants his opinion she will
ask for it thank you Mr. Finlay

he an onion in her pot

the fine lines she draws
around him fans herself
with judgments & dovegray pinions
she isn't waiting for the trumpet
that's for sure

says it's not a menagerie she's running
the world is too full of strumpets
yet she has made him
a little bird of a man
afraid even to molt

is this it
is this what i do
furnish him with a brass apartment
& every morning ask him
some stupid bird to sing
when i pull the hood off

wonder if
    the meek will
  ever inherit
a blessed thing

can't help thinking
Paul   his fist
full   of flowers
big burly ones
sun flowers id expect
or little fellas
butter cups perhaps
the way words   bend &
stammer on their stems

it is an anthology he brings
goofy grin on his face sings
me complete
with poesies & harebells
could be 'cowboy with guitar'
one of philip's

hi phil i brung yuh
sum flowers

p dreams
    the sky is a canvas
    reaches up & pulls
    down with a whump

  screen on which he is showing
  the latest attractions
    or coming
he is not sure which
garden movies in technicolour
and steve is pointing and laughing
looket the big skinny birds

watches himself as he dips & brushes
sky into a box of deep cobalt
and under it earth becomes
    a long bright smear
  justlikethat turns green
onto it dribbles purple & mauve

    and over that or in it
he spatters a patch of intense yellow
  dabs blue
    softer and almost powdered
blows white wisps over it all
and in it above everything
sets a cup wet with light
grins sheepishly when he says
it's pastoral   /his work

    philip the maker
    turns the fields

bright in flax and mustard
makes the world run blue with water
smiles as he rinses dust off the canvas
does one corner in small greens & then
        adds yellow spots

                                        frogs he says

since when i say   apparently
                                forever he says or seems to say
but there they are
            singing their little hearts out
            their voices are filled with sin & they
            rise from their throats in pastel arcs

                                and then he reaches
            just behind them puts
                a thick string in the grass
                    one final quirky move

my god how does he do it
the vast sweep of sky & earth
& anything else scarcely there barely alive

the light i cannot see how could there be such light
the world hurled in a light like no other light

so translucent you cannot believe what you have found there inside it the
 straight lines a dark purple that could have been drawn with ruler & ink
the poles stand up pitifully before a sky so undisturbed so forever it
cannot have noticed an empty heaven and they stand there tight-
shouldered & unjoined the wires missing there are no wires and they
silent as stone in unmoving joints & arms crossed where thousands have
hung and died a scale so spare there is no sparing anyone and though
they are coming at you past you will shove right out of the bottom left
corner have already moved past they do not see you have nothing to do
with you no nor with one another they have lost their line they appear
here & there on the page & wait as if there were no others do not even
notice the silhouettes all there is of us in lines filled a few small buildings
where they flip-flop onto the pool he has poured onto the surface like
spilled tea they could if they could see might see themselves in though it
stuns me to watch i can hardly breathe knowing now what he sees there is
nobody there nothing moving i cannot see anybody not even el greco
only the tiny rectangles of light the windows so small & so small in the
pond i wonder if anybody could be there in all the world a stark geometry
hard shapes and shadows cold & clear the entire creation so vacant you
wouldn't notice if if a sparrow flew in or if i were to call would it startle &
would anyone hear all that light humming as if is about to end

night its chocolate
                perks me

scritch   skri**tt**ssh

                                skr**it**sssh
                    sk*r*ritch
skrit_{SCHH}

                skr^{ish} ^{rits}sh

me a pen the paper smooth as beans
—cool when first I get it out
I can smell the cold in it—
on my fingers my face
a lamp the smooth brown table

                so quiet I hear the fire
                    ticking in the stove
                        taking its time
                    dreams that tremour El Greco
                    low thunder on the horizon
                            & lightning
                        he makes small sounds
                    cold clicking at the pane

all the things I dare not say
    scarcely think during day
        no not falling out
onto the page, not that

    little squiggles of ink my pen
    uncovers, kicks the snow off

feel like a chicken
all the words I need somewhere
under the snow the nib
scratches off   foots away
kicks it horny-toed bright-
eyed away **puckkk pukkk ppuKk**

oh that's me all right
foot loose & fancy free

may when I find them feed on them
wad them at the window against the cold
might spread them thick as rumours
fill the town's ear with them
bushels of rumours pour some
in p.'s ear if need be
seed it like a garden
matted with russian thistle
bristly as pigs
snout

by the gosh i just waltzed him
right clean through the prairie
just as smart as you please
     no if's and's or maybe's
right straight through the eyes
hopping round us
more hopeful than frogs in rain
snappy as buttons popping

boy oh boy we were going
to set the bottom of the world on fire
the prairie too if i had
anything to say about it
we were going to scorch it good

                                          sun whinnies
sun shinnies up the sky
                      wishes for running
          lights shining passage over waters
          a stunned & sinning man given to
                simile also to smiling & so
          inclined when people almost snap
                      their lives of overheated pyrex
          the brightly-coloured & paisley para
          sols round the sun where they squeeze like spandex
          pericardia wound round their tough red
          rubber souls provide shade
                                    no sky can contain
          not though i wait in my parapet handkerchief in hand

                the globe sheds night & day
                      slides off in rain
                shrugs off sun slides by
                more & more smooth
                it is a matter
                            when it comes down
        to it
                            a matter of para
            pluie he says it is plain
                            to see as anyone can it is parapluie
to the strain of rain the rattle of water in coalbucket lives
he might include talk in that   /the patter that is
            everywhere we find a para
-taxis -site -pet -llel -dox -lax -keet -clete -noia -nomasia
-plegia this the figure we are able to sit beside or behind
                            or at & eat
waiting for the parachute that lets us out lets us down

        pail in hand and searching for water

                    he is afraid
          here on the alkaline flats
                    he will not finish his para
          graph the world will (or will
                         not) rain on his para
               de his para
                              dise he rolls when he is set
          alongside beside the bed
               side sighs to one side of
                                   sighted there
          feeling slighted   /slightly,

          never fear she says de rien
          c'est bien it is to the sun
          & rain we belong we long to
          rain over us more & more
          we will find amore sooner
          or later arrive at mort
          uary oh aint you merry
          forget the wan & wary
          what in the end does it matter

          we could ever & always
          keep a paramour a para
          keet feet wet in the streets running
          with rain do everything we can
          try our level best never fail
          to clutter the gutters with glamorous flesh

goin' down the road that's what
Paul on the way
the brutal sunshine
falls on him in avalanche

can see him on Harlequin
leg cocked ear cocked
how foolish he is

there he goes reins in hand
head sloshed full with words
they must bump together loud as luggage in the hold
when he brings them these parcels of language
delivers them by hand   in person
& they've broken the bands the hands
they're slashed open

what does he think
I'm some kind of cowgirl
gangly with freckles
can't wait to hitch a ride
can't wait for ~~delivery~~ deliverance

thinks he is on an adventure
wants me to believe
he is an adventure i
will call him from call to him
from the steps my marriage sits on

take me
with you
why don't you
don't let me
languish

SSss   Paul
its not so useless eh
come in, come on
   give me the word why don't you
   me im sick & tired of this anguish

                              would be a siren
                              risen on heat
                              a red rinse in you

                  it's high noon
                  i can take the reins
                  i can make music
                  i can play for you Paul

                  we can make music
                  if you play with me

                  all you gotta do
                     is send me
                  a little sum thin
                  all i want is you
                          to give me
                  the word deliver the goods
                  so what on earth 's
                     keepin' yuh
                  hand it over big fella
                     ill sign for it
                                    /right here

they're looking at us
right now
over there
no no not there
/ there
ok so it's not a full house
but there're still one or two
two's better than nothing

yeah no they're there all right
just can't see them for the lights
but they're out there   /they're watching
& they think they got us to rights

no no not here
/there
look over there

yeah there on the edge

gawking & snuffling?
/ those two
those guys in the corner
looking at their watches?

those ghastly faces
on the other side
that's them

that's them &

they got an eye on us
they're itching for action
the whole kit & kaboodle
the whole shootin' works

　　　　　　　　look the wrong way &
　　　　　that's it it's lights out for us

& i don't mean maybe

I myself feel i am in
a wet towel i can't get
out of & you go crazy

other times it's a wounded
calf or lame one in these stories
Paul so dapper on his way in his way
on the pony constant his stories
the source & roots he rounds up
the crazy strays he stirs up
our talk prickly as the prairie

feels funny to be so herded so branded
the cowboy consonants what little air is left
the dipper full of sounds he drinks
with the back of his arm wiping his forehead

as for me & my words
we are buffeted on wind
don't worry about us we're ok
we puff on our passion
blow past in a fashion
tormented by dust & insects

you'd think we'd learn
throw in the towel
but no I still
wince when your words hit
peonies wilt
in the heart its sudden heat
turns us brown as pennies
under the train
its eye stares into us

the sharp pain the scars
i learn to bear listening
every night
under the big dipper riding
the prairie stinging in your heart

fair enough the brands i learn
to bear & sometimes flaunt
when they ask do I play
                    i be
come a fool for love
let go on the piano

Whump Whump my heart
my lungs thump away
i think some
times must be diapers
or pillow cases sun irons
out all their creases
all their worries &

the helter of grasshoppers
hoping to get in on the dance
little lawnmowers
whirring away inside me
to beat the band

listen listen to this philip
the man is saying
listen I'm all ears he says
it's the end of an ear
practically, plain & simple
no two ways about it
leans over & talks with the pigs
flies hang on his every word
he's got them buffaloed, put near, the flies

Philip kicks the rails
uh-huh uh-huh uh-huh
oh yeah
don' say

midst of all that
my long slow stroke
the paper I keep by my
self the paper I keep me in

what you say broken underfoot
crunch of seashells we walk on
the hens gather in excited talk
the nightyard broken open till
you feel like Venus herself
you now can see
they go in hard
clicks & pops
could
be in
high
heels
clickety
past

                    clickety
                     fast
                    click
                     ety
                                    clack
                    clam
                    orou
                    s as
                      a
                    train
keening into a glamorous
              sunset

                                    listen to that
                        would you just listen to that

this is what they do
in my diary they are
more lovely than
the way you twitter
more pure than your love
of whiteness this
paper & dairy & clippety-clop

w^whh_{yy}AAA you shout h'y**aa**
yuh little critters
which when they breathe give up
spumes of steam

why didn't you tell me
this before you had an eye
for the heifers plain & simple
pressing the flesh
p. you & your big hairy mitts
big silly grin
hung like a lantern from your face

                    people:
          bright thistles
          lighter than plums
          their aches streak the canvas
          where they are
          daubed in a few
          quick strokes

the hardest thing we do
gathering the end into ourselves

          wind tumbles
we tumble inside
we are turning to thistle
learning to be vacant
more empty than wind

when sun hits
the earth the west
explodes against the barn
viscous with yellow & red &
i know i am novitiate of love

birds before they are feathers
fall out of the nest & splash
on the air onto the ground

the stutter of telephone poles
their severe braille
& afterward
the drying

scabrous I would like to say
except Philip
voice almost vicious
would only say
wasn't I being   a little poetic
a little splashy he might on another occasion have claimed
though he himself is prepared to splot a little paint around

meanwhile I can hear
can hardly bear
the pigeons in your blood
a whole slew of gadgets
paul calls words, philip too
all of them whirring & cutting

what a way to come a courting
something to vitiate the day
where it lays big and white
newly laid

easy does it &
      cowpoke
           takes it
slow
       so slow

    birds on bare hills
feathers hanging down in ears
  bow & strut strut & bow
  hightoe their way to love

    says aww
       Phil this is for the birds

    oh strange poky man
      let's doesie doe

    let's a lemain left
      & sweet doesie doe

    let's alemain right
      let's mosey slow

    oh long-legged crow
      let's do it too

    oh alla man   right let's
      do it now

preacher jill paul calls her, the crow, the over-reacher
when into the highest-ceilinged night crow calls & calls
is that all Paul you're a fine one to talk
you with your letters and beginnings

                              crow goes out
            on a limb for us
                          crow climbs
            up light up dark crow
          bars things open

            takes things on
        her shoulder a bulgey moon
                      pushed out of joint
      so sugary & so out of place surgery seems inevitable

says :   **nope**   ee-**yup**

                                          nope
                crow talks   till she's blue

crow nests in the thorniest tree
shouts the reddest hunger she's ever heard
the screams that pass through
the terror she casts onto wind

crow cannot rest goes
                          up &
                                  down

        up
              down
on her toes knees shoulder
keeping time doing her part
to keep the whole works
from pulling apart & shutting down

crow pulls her lungs inside out
tears off her breath in comic balloon talk

crow feels jilted & she swears
she can put an end to things   /and will
curses the cold calls down the heat
hacks & spits on the lilacs
    shits on the crocus
when briefly they appear
calls down the sky because
it is the sky & because
it does not snuff up with clouds

cries because though co
    piously she calls
& calls night & day no one is there
when she sings the world's distress
no one hears & no one weeps

wwrrhhk

                                        wrrhhk
                        walk thru weeds & stubble

scatter of
            grasshoppers
                                    paper rubbing
                against sun

            heat stumbles/
                    fields behind drifting
                long tongues of dust
                            licking their neck & arms
            storms of gasses
                                    fenders so hot
                        they cant touch
                & all the while some
            one on a one-way
                                    is pulling
                    the field
                            a black skirt
                    shut behind
                                    the blotchy skin
                disappearing

                            the sky is kerosene
                            the sun chips on flint

                smell of graveldust
            where cars move like flies
                            sun
                heaves
            onto the other side
                        a glob of napalm/
                                        burning

spurred by your urgings
would rather I would dance
stiff as a hymn, as prim
pruned to keep from weeping
grief loud & lumpy as plums
when it falls **plop** at our feet
　　thick with purple

would rather I was a hymnary
you could hold in your arms
all the pain folded like rain is in rhyme
and i am turning to paper inside your book
　　　　under such circum
　　　stance the both of us one
　　　-legged crows trying
　　　　　to keep time
　　　stop it from overrunning
　　　　　us trying to fly

why when we lie together
am i wrestling with an angel
why do i feel both spurned & held
why do you yourself withhold
leave my side wide awake all night
long my thighs burning

wonder when you saddle up
in toothy grin and sidle
　　　　　why you talk of giving
me a sweet bridle you call a bridal suite
i could scrub till both of us are calloused

　　　　when i want only
　　for you what i want myself

        wish you an open heart
& chickens every spring & fall
ones that would fly out of their floppiness
spread onto the four winds full as out
-of-breath trains, coughing in & out of town
ashes from an ashtray maybe, I don't know

        the clouds spattering behind
                heart a blouse blown open
        house whose doors are knocked
        clean off their hinges
                        you & me on one
        of our binges
                sun a candy some kid could suck

initially it was good they said
　　　　　from alpha to omega they hoped
　　　　　pioneers scribbled themselves all over
　　　　　　　　into the place
　　　　　printed their impatience on quarters
　　　　　their names laid out in land offices
　　　　　they were entitled, had title
　　　　　　　　　　fair & square
　　　was it only a ruse mere convenience
　　　　　when they claimed their kids
　　　　　　　　　　　　imprinted on blue
　　　　　blankets suns that rose
　　　　　　　like bowling
　　　balls rolled into the stars &
　　　　　scattered them

　　　　　　　　　　& from my hand
　　　　　　　　　　　　a fountain
　　　　　flows the pen runs
　　　　　into creeks & eddies, splashing
　　　　　　oodles & oodles i mean
　　　　　　　they get a lot of ink
　　　　where it enters a thousand
　　　　potholes I puddle through day
　　　　dream where I stop & stir

　　　　　　　　can't help staring when I look
　　　　　　　　　back where I've stepped
　　　　the snowwhite floors of my mind
　　　my goodness how embarrassing did I do that
　　　thoughts in muddy boots tracking behind

　　　can't help thinking how like
　　　amulets they look

                                        i am you
                                     you are me

                    come lets
                    have a look
                    lets sing a song
                          a song of
                    capulets & couples
                    couples & couplets

                                      let's
                      sing along
            line filled with trains
            music of their confusion
            the wooden flowers they stop at
            drinking, take to stave off
            loneliness
                      they pull all day long
            the long days passing through
            the fire behind them & at night
            when they cross something they know
                                they got to emit it, passing

121

the bentleys

                               the playbill says you say
                          well you are looking for someone
                              it's not easy you want
someone to play the part
partly you do partly you don't
you move with the grace of a
duckbilled platypus monsieur directeur

       man with a megaphone
          hurt my ears when
               you shout *non non non*
the wooden rooms of your mind loud with echo
you have stacked applause painted it with expectancy
               never mind you are
supposed to be
          in love you've got
                          something to prove it's a matter
                          of audacity you are supposed to
                          really kiss him you've got
                          what it takes believe me
                          you have no choice
                          the curtain's up the lights are up
                                    you've got to
                               press the point
                          on him impress him
                          & the audience the audience
                          is listening you know it is
                          which though it has made none
                          is full of reservations & so it stirs & coughs
                          many talk among themselves, restless
                          dozens of grasshoppers muffled & amplified

every time you say
the same thing seek to hurl me
into lines you supply
efficient as a merchant sea captain
running contraband
i myself cannot accept

you on a mission you yourself a holy terror
words from the apostles themselves
what they say burning brand
new holes in your hands and mouth
this'll get them if anything does
                you say and toss
them up shout loud as throstles
                whatever they say

though they could be red as poppies are
in fact they are nothing but thistles you say
enough to throttle a threshing machine
    nothing but thorns & pricks
the man 's a poseur slick as an otter he is
                                a terrible imp
oster says the moon is his

trust him and you should
tell him what he needs to hear

                this'll have to do this'll
show him him and his thirst
his whistles & whiskers
no more than a runover christly porcupine
his talk of pater noster
does he mean it as threat
husky way he whispers
wet voice in the ear

                this is a tryst i know that
listen this is a him
you have to trust me on this p
these dreams of peter &
his tassles his black
& bristly nostrils say too bad

ttkk tkk thk ttk what's he doing
                    what's he up to now
                              putting you on
like this once more putting you on
              a pedestal still him & his
         he says i haven't seen
anything yet just watch him he can
pedal a lot faster and he bristles
         shoves his chin petulant as a child
              says he can make you
    immortal honest to god he can
though immoral is more like it
con fuses muss and muscle mixes thrush and thrust

ouch you say once he tries to reach

hi he says you could grow attached to that
         to him that is
though we both know it would be hard
you really could if only you would

                    you should ponder it in his heart
              there under the trestle where it shakes
                        a machine on full load

                        where the train shrieks
              if only you would play his part

the unsheltered rooms we move in & out of
wind more sullen than anything

    shattered skies
    clouds rattle in
    loud screams of rain
    sound of trains trying to stop

    how it must hurt
    so long not happening & now

long cranes hurl swiftly
the long careen of their calls
spot the gray canvas
are struck into day
      like nails

    pin us there
          drying, feel
    dry grass rubbing together
    we will remember the rest of our lives

    how wretched
         how wrenched
    she would be with breath
    your hands drenched

rain slashing the places
loneliness goes to hide
the way it watches you
pulling at its fingers
& talking to itself

                              yes p. your hands i wish
                              splashing all around
                              & in me techni-colour
                              wet like a painter
                              you could lay it
                              on thick

rocks in the fields
dreaming laconics
round as vowels
the constant winds
full of flapping & grit

feel   like a tea bag
steep   quietly in may
sun a warm   pot

kitchen a   bottle
sun talks   in stillness
falls in   soft colours
talks gently   on the table
in   my hands
where they   remember

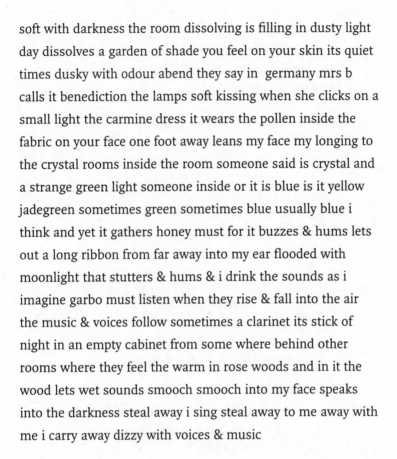

soft with darkness the room dissolving is filling in dusty light
day dissolves a garden of shade you feel on your skin its quiet
times dusky with odour abend they say in germany mrs b
calls it benediction the lamps soft kissing when she clicks on a
small light the carmine dress it wears the pollen inside the
fabric on your face one foot away leans my face my longing to
the crystal rooms inside the room someone said is crystal and
a strange green light someone inside or it is blue is it yellow
jadegreen sometimes green sometimes blue usually blue i
think and yet it gathers honey must for it buzzes & hums lets
out a long ribbon from far away into my ear flooded with
moonlight that stutters & hums & i drink the sounds as i
imagine garbo must listen when they rise & fall into the air
the music & voices follow sometimes a clarinet its stick of
night in an empty cabinet from some where behind other
rooms where they feel the warm in rose woods and in it the
wood lets wet sounds smooch smooch into my face speaks
into the darkness steal away i sing steal away to me away with
me i carry away dizzy with voices & music

though he is bound & determined
my husband is to have me
near and housebound where he will keep me
in the dark til i am horseblind

to hell with the preacher and the school master
once sunday

school 's out

that's it 'mouta here
im inta trance into dance
me im takin up
with handsome men

i really am

from here on it's miss
spelling and bad
grammar all the way
ive had it
up to here with detention and homework

listen/

think im kidding
they won't see me for lust
won't recognize me in the strange pun
chew aye shun when i write home from far
away places
without the least trace of compunction
without the smallest mention of the cat

could be one of the camenae
there in a small shelter
this side of the rise
this side of morning
   light   / shadow
                clouds scudding
  light & the shape of light
sliding over me like a camisole
fine and thin as cambric it would feel

like your camel's hair brush philip
and it would shimmer & it would
shimmy most certainly would
      like a chemise
you can see clean through

camisado if you aren't careful

& then another
man or the same one
i cannot tell
a long man shaking
some thing from his hand
falls into the grass and green
stalks whoosh flowers pop
open like speech in comic books
round thots
man with wand wanting some
thing lying there i ache i
arch like a swan
drink & drink the water

gol darn sandhill cranes again
who in their croon & nibbly toes
pull the sun closed behind them
in creases tuck the day in for the night
click unwanted mail back into the box
days we rent from the post office

faint whistle they make at the end
swaggery as young men at a dance

always trying to lower herself
into electricity how prosperous
    the blue pool
at first a slur in the sky bleaching
& a fizz a Viennese
walz only sharper

she herself would turn
her laughing toward him
a dizziness election brings

at the window sun would
glide in slide off she would
                    watch the sliding
                        the day the days
                porous & shining with music
rocking by, kids on a see-saw
their calcium moments

i can see bubbles children blow from their hands
the skin coloured to bursting
            talk about playing it
                  by ear

the breath running through
the bodies soft openings
no no wait listen what's that
                no one must hear
    sounds coming
        now & now & now a
            lone for a
        moment to
                    gether we play
                        a sweet swift tune
                    the swift hot seed
            smooth & hot as mustard
        loving the feel of the words in my mouth

there between the tall red bin
the grain cars rusted & empty

i leave my heart where it's skipped
a beat our bodies heat

letters laid in the grass like ancient runes
and everywhere the distant skirl of bagpipes their terrible
grief & longing

&
　　　　　　　　then the
　　　　spatter of am
　　　　　　　　　　pers ands
spitting on everyone's feet
　　　many fear
　　　　　　when they open

　　　their purses
　　　　　knowing the world
is full of ungrateful persons especially
　　　　　on saturday nights when
the parson is putting together sermons &
　　　　　　　　sends them
out on foolish err
　　　　　　ands their arms waving am
　　per sands running
　　　　out on them it's out
-and-out running around
& if they didn't feel well
coordinated they would feel as if they were
　　　　　tied up in nots

to tell the truth person
ally id say its not good
　　　it's not looking good
　　　　　　　　not when they
　　　　speck
le the page the side

walk with rain drops
create splots in dust
this is not how it is supposed to be
no wonder they are surprised
they are out of school
allowed to scribble anywhere
they want on summer

sometimes feel as though
                              i am a kid
                drawing my best intentions/ smudged
sun a big bruiser rains down on
                ruins every day

    my clearest thought daubed in crayola smears
        lost in leaky water colours
    a dabble here a dribble there
    double moustachios on gods face
                        a purple drool

                        naw he says you got it all wrong
                            the perspective it's all wrong
                            that there that's just doodling
                                look at those flowers
                                looket how they open
                                        their eyes
cough & you got powder   /all over the floor
all over yr face you could come down
                you aren't careful
either you got an armory or a dressing table
                    one or the other
those tippy flowers sneeze & thats it

                    sees the look on my face says
                    that spatter thats pontilism

                    well id say i seen flowers in their time
                                        /plenty
                    we seen them faces presst
                    against windows breath fogging
                    the daisies hogging the light & wanting
                    more something more

to happen the pages
they are turning
under turning away
into their papers proper as anything
you can't beat that i say

nope he says that's not bad but
that that's not
the way it is in case
i hadn't noticed
the lilacs how vile they are
their purple breath he meant
to say on the way in we saw people
bloated and red-faced didn't we
well they are peonies i of all people should see that
& call myself a gardener a pioneer i mean
there they are puffy with disaster their thin legs about
to snap
apt to take a
duster because
they themselves are too
heavy with their scarlet
sins aren't they

don't take his word for it
i could see for myself
the weedy graffiti everywhere
their brains
had clogged with guilt
wasn't the sun the very sun itself
dense with blood

           bodies thrown against the fences
     whapedahwhap whapedahwhap
     whapedahwhap   this is what
happens (on the edge of town)
everything sticks & stutters

            shadow /
                    light

     shadow / *light*

men whose ribs stick out
brittle as rickets click past

they must sound something
like the crown & anchor at the fair
spectral as celluloid in the movies
except you can see their eyes

                upon an ocean of sun
          pebbles grow eyes big as pueblos
          their faces fall into your face
          men on picket lines or boxcars
          their eyes which never entered
          the march of time never made it
          to the saturday newsreels ever

every night at the end when
people depart they move in the shallows
                              just goes to show
    the auditorium dissolves from too much
          light my heart clatters inside chairs
            it rattles & slaps shut & i stumble
       over footlights slip on burnout cigarettes
drawn into darkness the white flash of headlights

come to admire the sun a platinum blonde
stars every morning gasp & drown

evening grinds in the separator
soft snap of cards a baby
sudden cry of night a woman
or a man
a phone calling from its box the sewing
machine speeds like a frightened heart the frames
whir & click the machine throws them
onto a gray film in her head once
in awhile it hears
a dog staring at the road
scratching at the door
eyes poked out where have they gone
the houses sink into their missing
their feet fill up with resignation
the stink of ragweed and thistle
rooms where they hold hands
old albums in their minds

That's it
it's all
over isn't it
all over the place then
Over? What do you
mean: over?
it's all down
hill gone van
i shed disapp
eared kaput one
might say it's come
undone that is un
done it's come come
pleatly apart
nothing but
a ript & terri
ble fabric
ation a big fib
its so bia
sed c'est finis
& yet not not yet
not quite fini
shed it's lacking so
mething isn't
it & yet it is
finis hed said
is it really

is it all over

the place

it's a sad state a sad affair
he said she said
they wanted to ask
are you quite finished
shed say have you
finally had your say
come what may (this april or this
may) or may not end
is this any way
to say
it's over
to make it
a fait accompli
a fate worse than

hed copped out hadn't he
and to top that he'd lost his way
he was all over the place
& there was no way of stopping it
's all over
the piece & there
is no
way of stopping
is there
that's what
they're going to say
there 's no way
of stopping him
is there

it's never over
    it's never done is it
it never stops
   no matter what
you never forget
    those things
 do you

  hurry up she said
   it's time to let
    go it's time
  to get going it's time
   you were going
   give it up why don't you
 what more is there to say
  in the end what
     is there

 to say
except yes of course
you always could
there's always something
more in addition to make
up for who could
doubt it who could
say more or less
what you should
when it comes to that
there 's always something
    is this any way
    to say it's over
    is this the way
    it always ends

  well its a living
 isnt it its a living
    end

night after night lied
& Phyllis cried
out in the night
you could hear
frogs calling
through the spring
relentless way they sang
their hot green fever
slippery convulsion
under which Phyllis slept
& Phyllis wept

imagine the houses
that broke & the people
who fell out & left
people who gawk stupidly at you
you can see them now
as you drive past
empty-eyed

will no one come in
will no one look after them look
you can sit here where Paul played
cards played guitar played scholar played
footsie played the fool you can sit
here where Philip also played
preacher played possum played cuckold

& here is where Phyllis played
the organ played house kept
the plaid curtains clean & drawn
played the faith- & feck-less wife
here where Phyllis slept & wept

here is where no one played fair
& where all of them payed
in their dusty & reckless rooms

afterword :

think of the leakage
how they have escaped
the pages have fallen
open & there they are

bookmarks / pressed flowers
coffee stains dead mosquitoes
blemishes in paper & ink
signs of the past
leapt into a new book
they have a new look
have taken on an ant
erior life in ulterior
motives they intersect
the texts they alter & migrate between
that should mitigate against something

the seasons they pass in & out
ticket-sellers in a movie booth
players tossing cards & gathering
now is the shuffle of our discontent

the annoyance that here
when at last we dream of closing
running off in a flap
taking everything with us
the utter comfort of that illusion

someone should rip the page on us
spoil everything give away the ending
our emotions taken away from us

it's a cheap & transparent trick
such a stupid way to end

when all is
said & done
it really is
it's time to call

it quits